Chakras Demystified

Our True Communication System Revealed!

Monty Clayton Ritchings, FRC

Book #3 of The Embracing The Blend Series

ISBN: 978-1-7386347-9-8

Published by Monty C. Ritchings 2023

Surrey BC Canada

Check out my website for free tools for moving forward.

Dear Reader- Why You Should Read This Book

Chakras Demystified was written to help you to access information that will help you understand the validity and the value of accepting Chakras as part of the natural design of our being.

This book is written for people who do not necessarily have any depth of knowledge in the spiritual aspects of our existence. It is written in plain English, so you can understand and explore this exciting subject without having to download a "Spirituality to English" dictionary.

Once you have read this book and studied its contents, you will understand a whole new level of your existence, that was always there, and that you always used... but you did not realize it!

Chakras Demystified will support you in learning how to better manage your life on any level, once you understand that the Chakras are the most important communications system you have!

An Important Notice to Our Readers

Disclaimer

My dearest reader, I have written this book with the intention of assisting you by supplying some tools and information that I feel is pertinent to the process of revealing you to yourself.

I am a lay counselor and energetic healing practitioner long schooled in the art of living. According to those that make up the rules I am not a therapist. It does not matter to me what label is presented to identify me with others. I support all counseling practices that help individuals heal and empower themselves whether it be in the form of established counseling, energetic healing, yoga, etc. The only thing that matters to me is that you find your own light and express it.

With this in mind, I want to make it perfectly clear that this book is not meant to be a substitute for professional psychological help or any other form of intervention that may be deemed valuable or necessary in your healing journey. This statement is not meant to diminish the value of the information provided in this journal, or to diminish the value of the growth discovered by my clients with my assistance.

It is necessary, though, to have you recognize that the lessons procured through working your journey alone are more limiting than through external support.

I strongly urge you that as you work through the chapters and lessons in this book you obtain the support of a person capable of supporting you in your self-discovery. This book is intended as a guide for you, not a replacement for the help you may need.

Remember, a candle cannot light itself. My wish for you is that your inner light be illuminated in its own special way so that it adds to the overall light of all mankind.

Namaste

Monty Clayton Ritchings
September 2019

Table of Contents

Introduction

About the author

Other Books by Monty C. Ritchings

Chapter 1

Life

There is more to life than meets the eyes.

Until fairly recently in western society, it has seemed to be the norm to teach children to only trust what their parents can see.

So often, young children can see "beyond the veil". However, as soon as they start talking about their imaginary friends or other occurrences their parents cannot see, they are scolded for being stupid or told that it is just their imagination and that it is not real.

Slowly and sadly, the child shuts down their innate abilities to see the larger picture of our world and joins the 'reality' of the mundane world.

Later in life when this person attempts to see the unseeable, it remains just that; for the basic concepts that were given to them at the time of their birth have been overridden with much stronger belief systems that prevent their success.

Fortunately, in recent years, the inquiring minds of adults have become more open to the concept of a world beyond that of our physical eyes. People like Lee Carroll in his writings of his Kryon Series and his introduction of the concept of Indigo Children have started to change the fear based attitudes of people everywhere.

Children are now allowed to have their imaginary friends and even talk about formerly unspeakable occurrences.

Science is beginning to accept that the world is more than just a physical concept as well. They have even accepted that the atom, the basis of all physical life is composed of something. At least it is a start. Someday, hopefully soon, they will realize that quirks and quarks are still "made of something".

The reality is that everything that exists is composed of energy. Energy cannot be created or destroyed. It always is. It can only be transmuted or changed by a "scientific" process.

When a log on a fire burns, it is not destroyed. It is transmuted into a simpler, more basic form of energy form. That simpler form, carbon, eventually breaks down and returns to the soil that it originated from. The process goes on from there, continually repeating... energy transmuting into energy of another form... but always energy.

Log on fire..... carbon... soil.... tree... log on fire... carbon... soil......

Human beings, no matter how wonderful or evolved we are still, must comply with the laws of nature. We are composed of various elements of energy. These elements manifest into specific material (or immaterial) items that are designed to perform specific tasks and form a specific portion of the total composite who is this person.

Examples are parts of your body.

Every part of our body, physical and non-physical is created of a specific vibration of energy. Each organ is created of energy that vibrates at a specific frequency. That frequency can only produce that particular organ. Therefore, the vibration of the liver can only produce liver cells, it cannot produce an eyeball.

All living objects, animate and inanimate are composed of aspects that are created by these various frequencies. The energy of these vibrations emanate from them. This is what allows medical devices to observe them.

When you pop in for an MRI, this machine observes the vibration emanated from the observed organ, not the organ itself.

Unconsciously (for most people) we feel and interpret energetic information that is projected from one body to another. Still unconsciously, (for the most part) we react to this information.

This is called communication.

Chapter 2

Communication

When the mouth is open, true communication is rarely possible

Which tells you the truth about how someone feels about you? Being told "I love you" or being kissed?

The answer is obvious, isn't it!

The spoken work can be masked to hide the truth. It is also filtered by the receiver's own belief systems....

But a kiss! The truth is obvious... right through the receiver's own body.

Can you tell how someone feels about you by the way they hug you?

No matter what is said, you will know the truth, whether you like it or not.

Don't get me wrong, spoken communication is an important and valid form of communication. However, in order to get the whole story, one must pay attention to the body language that accompanies the verbiage.

The real truth comes from reading the non-verbal communication that is being expressed during the conversation. This information cannot be altered as much a one may try. Truth will always prevail!

As was explained in Chapter 1, everything is energy. When we communicate, we speak from many different levels of vibration. These are expressed through the body. We inherently pick up information through changes in facial expression, body stance, energy projection and hand movements during the verbal expression and after.

Putin!

President of Russia

What do you think he is really thinking?

Now you may wonder what all this has to do with Chakras. Bear with me and you will soon see how all this is related.

Reading energetic information from the body or body language, as it is commonly called, is an intuitive process. However, interpreting it is often perverted by the interpreter's belief systems that have developed over their lifetime through their own experiences.

In order to access the correct information, one needs to learn to be aware of how they block proper interpretation. This requires learning to be "body aware" or "self-aware".

A large percentage of our society has unconsciously chosen to disconnect from feeling their information processing systems in their bodies, as a form of self-protection. There have been too many hurts, so shutting down the connection to the body has become a requirement for survival. It is all about feeling "safe".

Unfortunately, this disconnection actually does exactly the opposite of the desired effect. Being able to access and interpret information the body communicates is vital to our survival and well-being.

Have you ever walked past a person and instantly become afraid... even though you have never interacted with this person?

Have you ever walked past a person and practically melted on the spot because you are so attracted to them?

These are perfect examples of how you already communicate nonverbally. Your unconscious mind picked up the information emanating from the other person, received it and interpreted it, all without you being consciously aware. Now that is communication!

This is also "true safety". In order to truly understand the situation one is currently in, they must be clearly open to receiving and correctly interpreting information from all sources.

Your energy field connected with their energy field, picked up the required information and gave you the necessary message. If you were to take the process further by interacting with these people, you would undoubtedly discover the truth about what you received.

In order to communicate non-verbally (both receiving and transmitting) effectively, one needs to be aware of their level of body awareness. The more open and aware one is, the more accurate the communication levels.

This process is a subject unto itself, so it will be dealt with at length in the next chapter, but suffice it to say for now, that in order to truly communicate, one must learn to relax through managed breathing and allow themselves to become reintegrated and at one with themselves.

The most important message here is that, if one wishes to get the complete message, it is essential that all communication systems be open and clear of blockages that can potentially alter the real truth.

Understanding how the body projects information through its various levels of energy is essential to effective communication. Being body aware, relaxed and open supports both the transmitting and receiving of information.

Now that we have a better understanding of the importance of non-verbal communication, let us move on to understanding what gets in the way of communication and how to reframe it.

Taking the time to be quiet regularly allows you to
be more integrated as a person.

Chapter 3

Learning to be Open

A book that is never opened cannot be read.

There is a theme to the message in this book.... Be open!!!!

We live what we believe!

If one is to be truly successful at being a good communicator, they must be open to send and receive messages clearly at any level.

Life does not work that way though... at least not easily. From the time we are conceived, we are bombarded with situations that require us to make decisions. Sometimes those decisions might have sounded good in the moment but in the long run they have been detrimental to our own best well-being and now limit the best expression of our life.

When these decisions are serious enough or repeated often enough, they become core beliefs, the beliefs that form the basis of our understanding of how our life will operate.

———

I hope you have noticed by now that there is not one person in your life who has been able to live a perfect life. Everybody gets bent about something. That bending causes a "warp" in our perception of the world. Until we recognize the "bent" belief it will continue to play out and skew our beliefs and our perceptions of information we receive and transmit that form our perception of our world.

Believe it or not, even our parents are not perfect! Here is an even scarier fact... parents are human too! They are as subject to the vagaries of life as we are.

Remember back a couple of chapters we were chatting about energy transmuting where the log became carbon, then soil and so on? Well this happens in belief systems as well.

For example parents 1 who lived way back in the 19th century travelled in a wagon across the United States to find their new home. The process was very long and arduous and fraught with danger and possible starvation.

From this situation these people developed a set of beliefs that life was very dangerous and that prosperity was not the norm, struggle and starvation was.

It was a very long trip lasting years as the progress was very slow. During the trip across America, parents 1 gave birth to several children that learned about life from their parents as they continued their journey. They learned that life was dangerous and that prosperity was not the norm. They learned to adapt to a world where going to bed hungry and scared was normal.

This family struggled even when they reached their destination. Life still was not easy. They had to build a home and constantly forage for food. They had to protect themselves from the natural elements and probably other people as well.

When the children of parents1 became older and married, they still carried the beliefs they had learned as children. Life was dangerous and prosperity was not the norm.

Life was far too demanding for any of these people to sit down and question their beliefs so they continued to struggle to survive, usually living just above starving.

Generations past and now we are six generations down the family tree, somewhere around the early 1950s. Let's look at the family now.

Dad has just got out of the army after coming back from fighting in Korea; the economy is weak so there are people struggling trying to feed the family. Mom has been busy trying to raise the kids while dad has been off to war. Neither parent has any social support so they do the best they can. They have no time to become aware of their belief systems. They are just trying to survive, and not doing well with it.

They have learned well that life is dangerous and prosperity is not the norm. It has now been thoroughly ingrained for at least seven generations.

Can you see how the energy (belief) keeps going through the same repetitious process over and over?

This belief system will continue, ad infinitum until such time as someone questions it and does what is required to change it.

The reason that it is comparable to the log...carbon...soil... tree analogy is because, the core belief has become so entrenched in the family belief system that it has become "natural" for them to believe and act accordingly just like a law of nature. Life is dangerous and prosperity is not the norm!

The belief continues to form and express ever and ever.

Have you ever taken the time to look at the beliefs that cause you to operate your life the way you do?

Psychologists claim that the rules we use to operate our life are over 80% entrenched by the time we are seven years old. We learned these rules by either interacting with other people, usually our caregivers or through direct life experiences.

We create the rules by making decisions about how we can best survive the situation we find ourselves in. Unfortunately for our older selves, these rules were decided by a child under the age of seven. This means the rules might not be adequate for the decisions we need to make as adults, but unless we are aware enough of this situation, we will continue to operate our lives in this manner basing our life decisions on decisions made as a child until the day we pass on.

These rules are held in the subconscious mind. When we find ourselves in an energetically familiar situation, the ego reaches into the unconscious library and extracts the beliefs that presumably are habitually required for this current situation.

You see, one of the main purposes of the ego is to protect you. And it does a great job... according to the rules it has learned as you survived your childhood.

Now that our society has sufficiently evolved to a point where we have a safety net in case of tragedy, we are now able to take the time to question and analyze the beliefs that motivate the outcomes in our individual lives... if we choose to.

That is a roundabout way of saying that we are now at a point in society where we have the opportunity to stop and have a look at how we operate our lives, and we have the tools and support to make those changes that can make our life better.

It is highly recommended that any individual who chooses to embark on a path of self –discovery find a verifiable support group, an individual counsellor and even a mentor to work with them as they dig through the depths of beliefs they have developed and integrated throughout their life.

Reframing your belief systems can be tough work and should not be entered into alone.

Working on your own can be; at least futile, and often dangerous until you become skilled at managing what comes up depending on how difficult life was for you as a child. The untrained mind cannot discern what is true or what is truly meant by the information that pops up. Be smart and get your support first.

Learning to be safe

The most important thing you can do for yourself as you begin to delve into your process of re-creation is to create safety for yourself. I truly hope you can do this in a manner that does not require medications or other limiting actions that may be counterproductive to your desire and best possible personal growth and health.

Assuming you are a reasonably mentally and emotionally healthy person, safety can be created by learning to relax, learning to breathe properly and separating yourself from the beliefs that you are working on. I will explain these.

Learning to relax is essential and is the first step in beginning the path of self-awareness. In order to relax, it is best to create a safe place for you to do your work, where you are unlikely to be distracted by other people or other annoyances that will keep you in the "outer" state.

Make the choice to be willing to let go and put aside any thoughts that may impede your ability to relax and focus on the task at hand. If the thoughts distracting you are too overwhelming, then either deal with them if possible or at least write them down so they will not feel they have been forgotten.

Sit somewhere comfortable with your back supported, hands in your lap and feet on the floor. This is preferable to lying down as it makes it easier for you to focus and not fall asleep when you let go.

As you move into the second stage which is breathing, move your focus onto your breath and away from the thoughts. Take deep breaths for a few moments and fill your body with fresh oxygen.

Make sure when you breathe you take full breaths causing the abdomen to rise. Hold the breath for a few seconds then slowly release. After a few minutes continue focusing on your breath but just breathe normally.

The third stage is one of the key points in learning to do personal growth work. Please understand and accept that:

You are not your body, mind, thoughts, emotions, life or anything else. You just are! I am!!!

This is very important when it comes to working with thoughts and emotions because you will not be able to let go and release or reframe the thought if you have an emotional attachment with the thought.

I had a friend years ago who suffered from fibromyalgia. She was consumed by this situation. Every minute of her day, the fibromyalgia was on her mind. She was consumed by trying to treat it. She went to fibromyalgia support groups. She dieted and did exercises. She did everything she could to deal with this situation... except one very important thing.

She did not let go. The fibromyalgia became part of her identity. It became part of her social network as she went to the support groups and made friends with other sufferers. It also gave validation to her existence and gave her an excuse to not really look at the underlying issues.

Please do not do this to yourself! If you truly want to be free you must recognize and accept that you are more than you can possibly see or know about yourself. You are much bigger than your body, mind, emotions, thoughts, etc. **I AM!!!!**

As you sit and focus on your breath allow yourself to relax into your chair. Continue focusing on the breath. Imagine a beautiful yellow sun above you and allow the feeling of that sun high in the sky to beam down on you filling you up with wonderful positive energy. Let it help you to relax even more.

When you are ready, open your eyes, take a final deep breath and carry on with your day.

It will take time to really relax. It will take time to learn to separate yourself from your thoughts and emotions. Be okay with this. It takes time to learn and accept any new belief system, especially one that challenges the old guard!

Your ego will fight this "invasive activity" as it undermines its perceived control over you. It will see relaxing as a threat because it will allow unwanted thoughts to enter your consciousness. However, eventually, when it realizes you are safe, it will settle down and work with you.

It is important to note here that you do not have to delve into or analyze thoughts that come up, just recognize them and let them go quietly.

Learning to relax will allow you to be more open and receptive.

Once you learn to be open energetically, you will become more aware and accepting of being consciously in your body. You will also become more aware of your own energy. As you become more aware and conscious of your energy, you will be able to feel the work of your chakras.

Feeling Your Aura

To start being energetically aware, you can experience feeling your "aura" (which is an "external" part of your body energy) by rubbing your hands together while briefly holding your breath, then as you breathe out hold your hands facing each other about 3 inches apart.

Focus on the palms of your hands and allow yourself to experience the feeling that has been created. It should feel like a warm magnetic feeling.

A Word of Caution

Some people believe that by opening yourself up energetically, you might be opening yourself to nefarious activity from the other side of the veil.

It is essential when creating safety that safety occurs on all your levels.

It is important not to poo poo this concern. If a person has concerns about such, then, to them, it is a real possibility.

We are multi-dimensional beings. We need to look after ourselves on all levels.

We are also incarnate beings (living inside a living, breathing body). That makes us king or queen of our roost.

WE HAVE ABSOLUTE DOMINION OVER OUR BEING.

No person or boogey man has more dominion than the soul inhabiting the body (that's you!). Therefore, no one or no thing can overpower another person and take over the body... unless that person, at some level chooses to allow it.

YOU ALWAYS HAVE DOMINION OVER YOURSELF!!

Creating Personal Safety

TO PROTECT ONESELF, ONE MUST FIRST BELIEVE THEY ARE TRULY SAFE.

After all, you are what you think and believe about yourself.

Secondly, the person must place themselves at a highest possible level of vibration. This is done, again by visualizing.

If you wish to protect yourself energetically, do this little visualization.

Breathe in deeply while visualizing gold energy flowing into the top of your head through an opening at the crown, filling your entire being and then emanating out of the body and filling the space all around your body for a distance of about four feet in any direction as you breathe out. Continue to do this until you feel yourself energized.

This exercise strengthens the energy field. Strongest energy field wins!

You can repeat "I am safe and protected" three times as you need as well. Good to let the mind help. This can be repeated any time it is desired.

It is important to understand that we are created safe by our nature. We have been trained out of our natural safety through our experiences in life. When you become really comfortable with feeling your own energy and being able to increase its levels, you will be in your natural safety as long as you continue to hold that belief in your mind.

Being protected is a different thing. It is an individual thing. Just make sure that you do not use any form of protection that separates you from your high energy.

For example, shutting yourself off energetically from the world in a given situation is a form of protection. It does not make you safe. Safety is being connected to divine source through your energy exercises and your true belief that you are safe.

I think at this point, we are sufficiently ready to begin to study Chakras. Just remember, you are completely responsible for how you create and manifest yourself in your world.

Chapter 4

Chakras

We finally get to the reason this book was written!

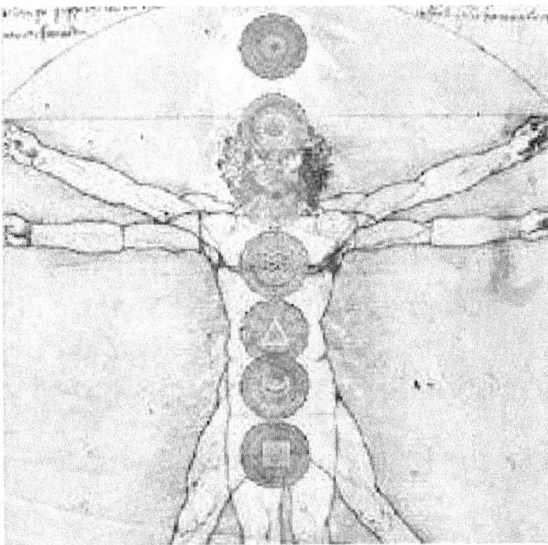

As I explained at the beginning of this book, Chakras are like hydro substations. They collect energy from a larger source (the universe) and process the energy into a specific frequency of vibration in order to communicate their individual message with the world.

Every living being has an energy field. Animals, plants, even the earth have an individual energy field. These energy fields are composed of various levels of energy which are differentiated by their frequency or rate of vibration.

The energies of the Chakras form the various layers of the aura.

The energy which is received and transmitted through the chakra vibrates at its own unique vibration. Nothing else ever vibrates at that frequency.

In a pure, uninhibited state, the aura expressing from a living being expresses itself in the colors of the rainbow. The colors in the layers of the aura are identical with the colors of the rainbow.

The higher the frequency of the vibration of the color, the further it projects beyond the body.

The Politics of Chakras

Before we actually get into the explanations of each of the Chakras, we have to deal with the politics. Yes, even Chakras are embroiled into fighting between different belief systems.

What I present to you, I believe to be true. I believe it to be true because it is what I have experienced and what I have been taught over my 30+ years of study and practice in the field of mysticism.

You are free to choose what you want to believe, though, so I will present both sides of the cases and you can choose what you wish to believe.

First of all, some people believe that every second chakra spins in the opposite direction of the chakras on either side. I believe they all spin in the same direction. Besides having physically experienced the feel of the rotations, there is a universal rule that every field of energy, in a healthy and vital state, rotates clockwise.

If a chakra is turning counter clockwise or even stalled, there is an issue going on that has caused that malfunction.

Secondly, some theorists claim that all of sudden the root chakra is now horizontal instead of vertical, as it has been for millions of years. My understanding is that the root chakra is the opposite end of the crown chakra, allowing energy to enter through one chakra and flow out through the other.

If the root chakra were to all of a sudden become horizontal, what would be the other end of the crown chakra?

Most important question: Why?

What would be the value of the root chakra becoming horizontal? The universe is never arbitrary, so there would need to be a valid reason for it to occur.

Have a look at the picture below. This is the accepted positioning of the seven major chakras. This is how we will explain them.

The five central chakras are horizontally positioned with a back and front "door" while the root chakra and crown chakra are vertical and each other's opposite end.

The Seven In-Body Chakras

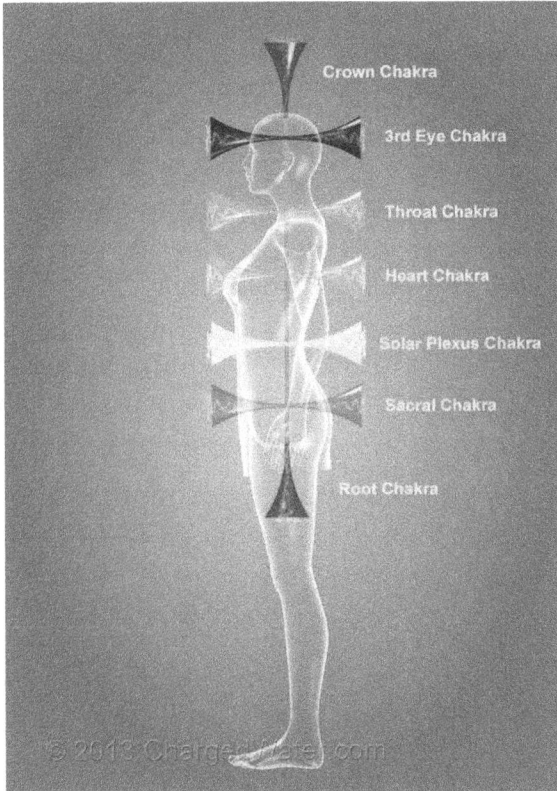

Crown Chakra

3rd Eye Chakra

Throat Chakra

Heart Chakra

Solar Plexus Chakra

Sacral Chakra

Root Chakra

© 2013 ChargedWater.com

The Seven In-Body Chakras

In most philosophies and esoteric thought organizations, the number of major chakras in the body of any living being is seven. There are two major chakras which are beyond the physical body but in the auric field which also are worthy of inclusion but will be explained separately.

When someone explains chakras, they are listed from the lowest frequency to highest.

This does not make any one chakra more important than another. After all, we do not compare the value of information given to us by a telephone call as being more important than information we got from a book. Information is information, no matter the origin.

We all function on all energetic levels at all times, as long as we are incarnate. It is only a matter of how we operate on each level that determines the quality and expression of that particular chakra.

For now, we will focus on explaining each of the individual major chakras. Later on, we will focus on what happens when life interferes.

The chakras are listed below from lowest frequency to the highest frequency.

The First Chakra- The Root

The root Chakra is located near the tip of the tailbone but is associated with the prostate gland in men and the ovaries in women. Its color is red.

Being that the Chakra is related to the prostate and ovaries, it is easily determined that this chakra is related to male energy and female energy in the physical form. This chakra is related to the maleness and femaleness of the individual and their ability to ground themselves to the earth and express themselves as sentient beings (since physical energy relates to earth energy). It is also the Chakra of family expression, which helps define the value of the energies of the masculine and feminine.

The Second Chakra- The Spleen or Sacral

The second Chakra is the Sacral Chakra, located in the spleen. The spleen is located on the left side of the lower abdomen behind the large intestines. The color of this chakra is orange.

The spleen is part of the body's immune system and works to keep metabolic balance throughout the physical being. The spleen is the chakra of personal power at the mental level. It relates to sexuality and personal magnetism. It also relates to how a person "digests" life.

The Third Chakra-The Solar Plexus

The third Chakra is located just below the base of the breast bone. It is related to the adrenals which sit on top of the kidneys. The solar plexus actually sits above the adrenals. Its color is yellow.

The purpose of this Chakra is twofold. First of all, it expresses the energy of activation. As the adrenals activate your body, the energy of this Chakra activates your life.

The solar plexus is also the seat of Universal Consciousness, and is the Chakra of highest vibration in relation to the physical plane.

The Fourth Chakra- The Heart

The Heart Chakra is located about 3 inches up the breastbone in the region of the heart. Its color is green.

This Chakra is the center of the body energetically. It is the point where the physical energy congregates with the etheric or spirit energy, the communion of spirit and body. It is the point where the energy for spiritual healing is based.

An important note about the energy of this Chakra-It is considered the Chakra of love. The truth is all positive energy is about love so, therefore, the energy for any of the chakras is about love.

The particular energy of love emitted by this chakra is not about romantic love. It is the energy of agape or universal love as when one gives from the heart.

The Fifth Chakra- The Thyroid Gland

The fifth Chakra is located in the center of the throat, behind the hollow space in the middle. The color of this Chakra is a rich deep blue.

This Chakra is located in the Thyroid Gland at the energetic point where the head energy connects with the body energy.

This chakra is the energy of communication to the mundane or outside world, as is the thyroid, the communication management center for the physical body. The thyroid gland manages and dispenses calcium into the nervous system. The calcium is the carrier of messages throughout the system.

The Sixth Chakra- The Third Eye

The sixth Chakra, commonly called the Third Eye, is located in the center of the forehead. It is actually located at this point but centrally in the brain in the Pineal Gland. The color of this Chakra is purple.

This Chakra is the point of the next higher level of communication, namely spiritual energy or intuitive energy. It is the basis of the sixth sense, which is included in the hypothalamus. Its color is purple.

The basic job of the pineal gland, and the third eye, is to provide information from beyond the physical world that is necessary to protect that person. It is how we read the energy of other beings so we intuitively know how to interact with them and be safe.

 A person can be trained to use this tool for work beyond their own safety by learning how to "see" energy and interpret it for the benefit of others.

The Seventh Chakra- The Crown

The Crown Chakra is located in the center of the brain as well, the difference being that it is a vertical Chakra as opposed to the sixth Chakra which is horizontal. Its color is violet.

The Crown Chakra is seated in the pituitary gland, the master gland of the physical body. Like the pituitary gland, it is the master Chakra. Its purpose is to manage all the energy of the body so that a sense of metabolic homeostasis is created, and maintained throughout on all energetic levels.

The Crown Chakra is the direct connection to the overall universal source. When a child is born, it has a "soft spot" at the top of the head. This is caused due to a separation between the two halves of the skull.

The purpose of this opening is to allow cosmic information to be downloaded into the pituitary gland, which, in turn is transmitted to the relevant location in the body. This information forms the basis of the life purpose and the tool kit this person will have access to while incarnate for developing and managing their own unique life.

It is also the entry point for the soul to enter the body as the first breath is taken at birth. Once the information has been downloaded, the halves of the skull grow together, usually being completed sometime before the person's seventh birthday.

It is also the exit point for the soul at last breath for once the Crown Chakra and pituitary gland surrender to death, the soul and the physical body separate.

Other important Chakras

The most important "other" Chakra is the thymus gland. It is located upper mid-chest above the bronchi. The thymus gland is part of the immune system management team.

It is commonly known as the "High Heart" Chakra. It is considered the seat of the inner child, expanding its energy through laughter. Its color is royal blue.

There is some debate about which is the real heart Chakra. Again, I reiterate, it is up to you. I feel they are kindred spirits of the same energy but serve slightly different purposes.

The Heart Chakra is more centered and therefore more grounded for healing purposes. The high heart is higher, so more connected to spirit energy and healing on a spiritual level.

In healing, there are also minor Chakras located in the elbows and knees that can be used to assist in managing the movement of energy along the limb.

The last minor Chakras are in the bottom of the feet. Their purpose is to work as a gateway, allowing the energy from the body to flow into the earth and vice versa.

The two sides of the Chakras

Each of the energy has two ends to it so that energy can flow in and flow out. It is my understanding that the energy flowing through the horizontal Chakras (2-6) enters the body through the opening in the back, and is transmitted through the front.

To me, this makes sense because the bulk of our communication is performed from the front of the body.

As we have said before, the Crown Chakra and the Root Chakra are opposites to each other. However, energy flows in either direction through the Chakras as sky energy flows into the body downward through the Crown Chakra, while the body receives and absorbs earth energy through the Root Chakra via the legs and feet.

The Nine Chakra System

The seven Chakra system only works with the energies of the Chakras in the physical body as we have discussed above.

In recent years, many of the metaphysical and mystical philosophies have realized that in teaching about the Chakras, there is an important need for us to realize and work holistically. We must, therefore, include the auric field as part of the sentient being's package.

A healthy human's aura expands about four feet beyond the visible body in any direction. (That is why you can feel other people when they move close to you.)

It is now recognized that two other points are also major Chakras, but resident only in the auric field. They are:

The Star Chakra. It is found about 18 inches directly above the Crown Chakra. It is the unique connection for the person between themselves and the universe. This energy because it comes from sky is considered positive in polarity.

The energy from the universe flows into the Star Chakra, then flows down into the Crown Chakra and into the body.

The Earth Chakra. It is found at the other end of the auric field, 18 inches below the earth. The purpose of this Chakra is to help the person ground themselves to the planet, just like roots to a plant. The polarity of the energy of this Chakra is negative.

One can make a comparison to explain the value of the Star Chakra and the Earth Chakra by comparing our body to an apple. The end of the apple that is connected to the tree has a negative polarity as it is pulling energy from the earth. The fly end of the apple is the positive end as it draws energy from the universe.

Now that we have completed our discussion on Chakras themselves, we can move onto how chakras work in our lives.

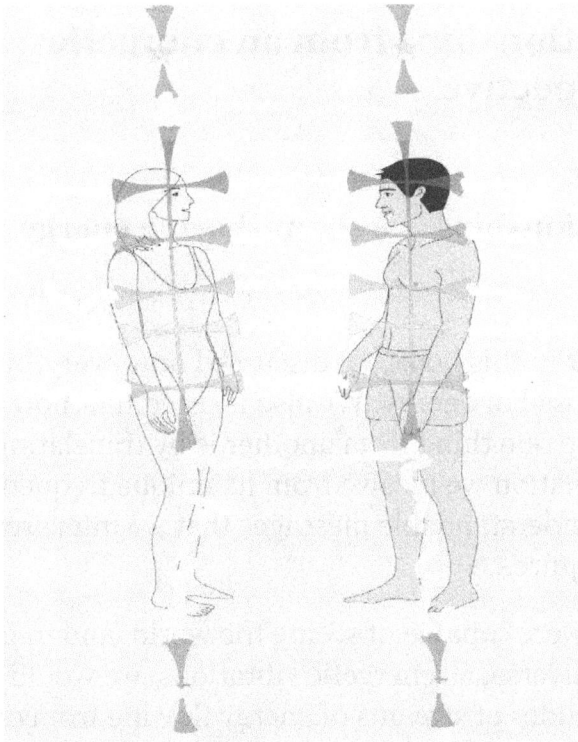

The Nine Chakra System including energetic interactions

Chapter 5

Relationships from an energetic perspective

Relationships are about sharing energy.

Earlier in this book, we discussed how everything is composed of energy. We also learned that how we discern one thing from another is by translating the information we receive from its unique frequency into understandable messages that we interpret as we require.

If we were capable of seeing the world, and in fact the universe, as energetic vibrations, we would see multitudes of streams of energy flowing from one object to another.

Everything that exists communicates by this means. However, we are only able to interpret information that is within a specific vibratory range. Can you imagine how overwhelmed our brains would be if we could receive and interpret all vibrations?

Our Chakras receive and transmit energy of specific frequencies. These frequencies are contained within the range of frequencies that we can interpret.

The purpose of this chapter is to discuss how relationships function from an energetic perspective.

When we interact with another person, our chakras automatically check them out. When the energies connect, information is transmitted and received to both people instantly. This information is interpreted by each person according to their personal belief systems, to instantly determine what kind of relationship might be available with this other person.

Have you ever entered a room full of people and been automatically attracted to one specific person? What did you feel? Where did you feel it in your body?

Have you ever run into a person and immediately felt negative energy from them, maybe so bad that you turned and removed yourself from the situation?

How do you feel when you encounter someone you know really well?

These are examples of your Chakras picking up information from the other person's chakras.

We only connect on certain levels of energy with each person we have relationships with. Depending on the depth of the relationship, this energetic bond can be very minimal or extremely deep.

Each relationship has an individual set of connections as well. This connection can change, but the first connection usually has the most impact on the long-term definition of the relationship.

The more Chakras that connect, the bigger the connection and, depending on the level of personal and spiritual development of the individuals, the more significant and conscious the relationship can be.

All people connect energetically in this manner; however, it depends largely on the "maturity" of the individuals to be able to recognize the Chakras they connect on and how they will manage the flow of energy between them.

After all, just because the two people connect on certain levels does not mean the relationship is relegated only to that certain connection.

Exploration by both parties regarding the feelings they perceive can redefine the parameters.

People who are not open or are not very developed spiritually will not connect very well with others in the upper Chakras. They will connect mostly on the lower three physical chakras.

People who are not very well connected to the earth will not connect well with the energy of others through the lower chakras but might with the upper Chakras. These people would be considered "not grounded", at least not in this particular relationship.

Depending on how the Chakras operate in each individual, the connections will vary as to how they are connected. It can also be influenced by how each individual is feeling at the time.

Two people who connect really well only on the highest chakras will have a great relationship doing altruistic activities or studying different subjects or enjoying meaningful conversations. They will not likely have any substantial kind of physical relationship.

Two people who connect very well at the lower Chakras might have a very physical relationship with a lot of mental and emotional activities, but they will not discuss great philosophical subjects or do spiritual healing together.

All of this is ok. Every relationship is unique and subject to change. We need to accept this fact and be ok that we cannot have meaningful conversations with some people,, and we cannot have sex with everybody. It just makes life much more interesting.

An interesting and important note to appreciate is that we do not connect with all people. We inherently have the automatic capacity to withhold our Chakra energy and only transmit it when a connection of value occurs.

This is so important because if we were to allow ourselves to connect with everyone, we would become very tired quickly from all the exertion. It would also be very hard to focus on tasks, as we would not be able to focus on what we were trying to do.

Chakra energy and core beliefs

As was mentioned in an earlier chapter, what our memories hold affects how our chakras operate.

We all have had traumatic lessons in our childhood. These lessons have caused us to make very serious decisions that may impact our perspective of life until the day we pass on.

In a perfectly spiritual person, all of their Chakras are open at the right level and receive and transmit information appropriately.... There are very few people on our planet like this today.

The rest of us live our lives having our Chakras opening and closing as we process our stuff. However, sometimes "our stuff" is too much; causing our mind and the related Chakra to make the choice to shut down or even cause the Chakra to revolve backwards on a long term basis.

This situation is or should be of great concern to people who suffer from this choice... and it is a choice!

By nature, our Chakras are open and happily turning continuously in a clockwise manner. People who have suffered events in their lives such as sexual and physical abuse or abandonment will find themselves struggling to allow their lower Chakras to be open.

People who struggle with feeling safe due to events that caused then to experience neglect or rejection will often struggle with issues related to their higher chakras. They will only believe in things they can see.

When Chakras are closed for extended periods of time, serious issues can develop in the person. The parts of the body related to the Chakra can become either seriously depleted or overloaded with energy that is not being allowed to process as designed. Prolonged lack of energetic balance cannot be sustained as the body will fight to regain metabolic balance.

Many of the conditions we suffer from over our lives are related to improper flow of energy through the Chakras. After all, everything that exists is energy in its own unique form and it always strives to maintain that form.

This fact is a key to understanding our health. The more open our Chakras are overall, the healthier we will express ourselves as an individual. Developing and maintaining a healthy mindset is an absolute must for good health... and it is rarely too late to start, even if your health is being challenged.

Relationship Issues

Until I get around to writing it, there is no book that explains the rules of life. Unfortunately for the world, it is not on my list of writing aspirations, so everyone will just have to keep limping along trying to figure it out for themselves.

I wrote a book several years ago called **Embracing The Blend**. Its focus is about core beliefs and how we learn relationships.

As I have said before, we learn the bulk of our core beliefs that form the structure of our belief systems and our life interpretation system prior to our seventh birthday.

One of the major lessons we learn, and it is a very slow lesson with many layers, is about how relationships work. We learn the rules mostly by watching our parents and somewhat less from other adults and our siblings that play in our lives.

We learn to be primarily one of four relationship characters:

- Like dad
- Like mom
- The opposite of dad
- The opposite of mom

If you watch yourself or any other person you know really well, look at how they do their relationships and see if you can pick out which character they have chosen.

For people like me, having had four parents as I grew up, it is a little difficult to pick out, but I definitely can see aspects of each of my parents as I evolve.

This is not cut and dried. You will pick up characteristics from other significant teachers, but there is always a primary character.

Now here is the part that makes this learning process really suck!

Mom and dad were not perfect! They had no better idea what they were doing than their parents did! Now the job is yours to figure it out!

In most childhoods, the person will be attracted to their opposite parent. Boys, especially, are really taught to be needy of their mother's attention while girls learn to rip their father's hearts out with their beautiful little eyes that entwine right around their father's brains.

So boys learn to grow up needing mommy's approval and girls learn to manipulate men by being cutesy. Then life intervenes!

Boys don't get enough of mommy's approval and daddy and other brothers compete for the limited amount of approval mommy has to dole out.

Girls find daddy working long hours to keep the family fed, so they feel neglected and unloved. When mommy tries to horn in on their territory, the rivalry starts.

This is exaggerated, but it is the world of relationships. As each child winds their way through their childhood, they learn how to build relationships by watching mommy and daddy and by doing whatever they feel they need to do to get their needs met.

All these lessons are contained in the subconscious mind. These lessons manage how each individual responds to their world around them. Their Chakras react to these beliefs.

Children who have to compete for a parent's attention and approval continuously will develop extra wide Chakra openings, so they can grab whatever energy they can get.

Children who are neglected, abused and otherwise mistreated may choose to close a particular Chakra in an attempt to preserve the energy.

It is all about safety!

This is why it is so important for children to be raised in an environment with two healthy loving parents who have the time, capacity and willingness to consciously raise the child to be healthy on any level as a person. It is the only way a child can grow up to be a fully functional adult without having to do a mess of emotional and mental reframing work.

When people interact with each other, they unconsciously attempt to link up the corresponding Chakra energy. Each person's energy "feels" the other person's energy system for commonality in need.

A girl might need a father figure, so is attracted to a boy who is really demonstrative of his manliness. The relationship is great... until the humans enter!

She finds out his manly façade is an illusion while he finds out she is not willing to give him enough mother energy.

Each individual struggles to have their needs met unconsciously. This causes an energy rivalry which boils over into the real world. Neither knows how to manage the situation to have their needs met and neither of them is capable of understanding what their partner's needs are.

As this is going on, the energy of the Chakras is going crazy trying to find satisfaction and fulfillment.

Finally, the relationship is a bust. She is off to somewhere else and so is he. Does it just end, and everyone carries on? Not likely?

Each of them has mentally and perhaps physically chosen to leave the relationship, but did they disconnect at the Chakra level?

The likelihood is no, they have not. Here are some likely outcomes:

- One will feel great emotional and possibly physical distress since the Chakra is not being fed as it desires. This can really physically hurt!

- One will run off into another relationship thus disconnecting from the first partner and immediately connecting with a new source of the required energy leaving the Chakras of the other flailing in the wind.

- One could feel very angry having their energy source revoked and do all kinds of stupid things that they will live to regret... like posting unkind things on Facebook or worse!

There may be more possible outcomes, but these will give you the idea.

The problem with this situation is the people involved in the relationship do not understand how we interact on an energetic level. They do not understand how we draw energy from others to satisfy our own needs and then feel like we are falling apart when the energy source disappears.

So what to do?

If people understood how we interact energetically and how the energies of each person are intertwined with each other, they could learn how to choose and manage relationships and more importantly learn how to manage their own energetic needs properly.

I think at this point we will leave this subject to a chapter of its own. So let's take a deep breath, forgive ourselves for not knowing all this stuff before we jump into relationships and get ready to create a new way of living.

Chapter 6

Working With Your Own Energy

Throughout this book, we have repeatedly been talking about universal energy and how everything is composed of this wonderful aspect of the Divine.

Like everything that exists, we expend energy and we need to recharge it. We need to eat. We need to drink water. We need to sleep, and we need to live our lives. All these things renew our energies on various levels. However, they do not have the ability to recharge the energy we need and use the most... our divine energy.

For what reason I do not know, but somewhere in the past, we seem to have forgotten that we are part of the divine essence. We are designed to recharge our divine self directly from Divine source.

Somewhere along the way, it became common to attempt to access our Divine energy through our interactions with other people or by having lovable pets to scratch their backs or rub their bellies. This process works as long as everything is perfect, but what a mess when things go sideways.

Just like in the example in the previous chapter, attempting to source this high level of energy from other people can come at a very great cost. So the question is "How do we do it without all the drama?"

It sounds simple, but the answer takes work. We need to reconnect with the Divine Source, with the Universal energy that is innate in our being. We need to learn to hold our connection with the universe constantly so that we are consistently replenished at this level.

There are many aspects to this process. We will go through each one so you can understand what needs to be done to feed yourself.

First of all, I feel that I must state emphatically that this process does not require a belief in any religious organization. These organizations are man-made and do not provide the necessary connection for this process.

It is important, though, to realize and accept that there is a greater consciousness than our own. I will refer to this as Divine Intelligence or Cosmic Consciousness, or maybe even God. However, please just accept that I am referring to the same point of source.

Secondly, it is important to realize and accept that we are a part of this source. We cannot opt out. We might choose to close our minds to this truth and not benefit from this extremely important aspect of ourselves, but it is there, no matter what.

Every level of energy that composes who we are is Divine Energy. By accepting this fact, we automatically open ourselves to the connection we have with Source.

The next step is to understand that we can manage our relationship with these various energies. In fact, we already do through our thoughts and belief systems.

As we have spoken about in previous chapters, our mind can open and close chakras instantly as suited by any particular belief we hold.

In that, it is absolutely essential that we be vigilant about our thoughts. We need to question everything we believe until we have reframed any thought that exists in our mind that separates us from our true selves and Divine Source.

This process may be scary. The ego (which has become highly overworked in our society) will resist change, but by carefully, consistently and lovingly learning tools to change your beliefs and your habits, you will consciously reconnect with the flow.

Working with a person who is well trained in helping you retrain yourself is absolutely essential. Programs like Core Belief Engineering are wonderful and safe tools for making the changes you desire.

Why do you want to do all this work?

Firstly, so you will feel absolutely great about your life no matter how it is flowing.

Secondly, because it is what you are here to do.

Thirdly, this is how Divine Consciousness grows. As you grow, it grows because it experiences through you... and everyone else.

Once you can get past your ego and your fears of change, you will find that everything in your life will improve.

Relationships will change too because once you learn to source your energy from the Divine Source, you will no longer be dependent on other people for your continual fix.

This does not mean that you will not want to have relationships; it only means that you will not **need** relationships any more than you need any other addiction. Your relationships will be by choice, not by need.

Relationships will become lighter, more fun, more meaningful, and will last longer. Does that make it worthwhile?

While we are working on the emotional/mental aspects of reconnecting with Source, there are exercises one can do to hasten the process. These are included in the next chapter.

I sincerely hope you are having fun with this bundle of information I have put together for you.

Chapter 7

Exercises for Working with Source

Now we get down to the fun!

The most important thing for you to accept during this process is that you are now doing what you naturally do anyway, only your ego based training is being set aside. These exercises are perfectly safe.

An important note to realize and accept when working with Divine energy is that you are raising your own energy to a higher level than you have known before. The higher the vibration you absorb and emanate, the safer you are. The reason for this is that one cannot hold victim energy, which is a low energy form in a high state of Universal or Divine Energy, as they are incompatible.

The first aspect we are going to look at is the physical. Working in the esoteric realm requires cooperation from the physical body and the physical environment in order to be able to relax and allow yourself to let go.

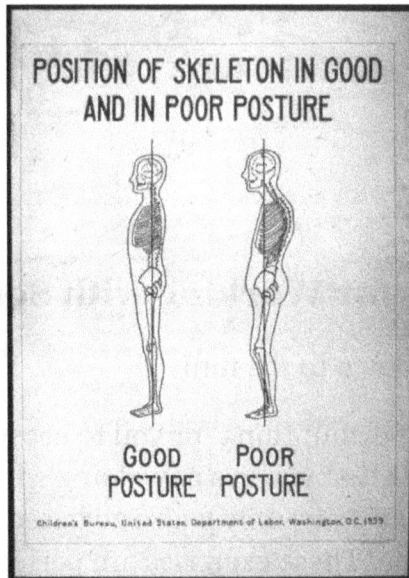

POSITION OF SKELETON IN GOOD AND IN POOR POSTURE

GOOD POSTURE   POOR POSTURE

Children's Bureau, United States, Department of Labor, Washington, D.C. 1939

You may have experienced yoga and some types of meditation. One of the first things they will say to you is that position is everything. I am going to explain why this is true.

As has been stated before, energy flows up and down the body through the nervous system. Sky energy flows in from the Star Chakra into the Crown Chakra and down the body into the earth and into the Earth Chakra, and vice versa.

In order for the energy to flow properly, it is imperative that the body be positioned properly.

This is not just true for allowing the energy to flow, it is imperative all the time. Correct posture is vital for proper body performance.

When the posture is correct, there is less resistance between the body parts and the internal flow of energy.

The most important concerns are holding your head over your shoulders so that your shoulders and neck are straight, not slumped or pushed forward. The reason physically for this is that correct posture takes the pressure off the muscles as they try to support the weight of the head. Energetically, the point in your neck where the cervical vertebrae connect to the Thoracic Vertebrae at the base of the neck is a point where the energy traveling up and down the spine can become blocked if this point is not open.

Have you ever heard of someone being called a "head case"?

This situation is caused by the flow of energy being cut off either at this point or if the Crown Chakra is closed, or both. The energy becomes trapped in the head.

The second aspect of focus is the alignment of the spine. The spine should be resting comfortably. Positioning of the spine is not meant to be punishment. However, it is necessary to keep the flow of energy moving up and down the body as easily as possible. A straight spine makes this easily accomplished.

Each of the Chakras is located in a specific organ or gland that is related to a specific vertebra in the spine. Incorrect posture will limit the flow of energy and may cause unnecessary discomfort.

When doing energy work, it is always preferable to be in a vertical or semi-vertical position, such as sitting. If you have difficulty in holding your back reasonably straight when you are sitting, place a cushion behind your back or find somewhere different to sit. You should also be able to place your feet squarely on the floor.

Lying flat during any kind of meditation or mental visualization process is acceptable, but not recommended because it is too easy to fall asleep and is harder to remain focused.

Next, important aspects in the physical.

1. Water. Being hydrated properly is essential. After all, we are primarily composed of water. The energy we are working with travels better in a hydrated body. Besides, it is easier to concentrate if you do not have a dry mouth.

2. Breathing. For some reason we, as humans, have forgotten how to breathe properly. We have become lazy in our breaths, and now are paying the price for it.

Most people seem to breathe using only the upper portion of their lungs. You can check yourself just by focusing on how you breathe mechanically. What is moving when you breathe?

If only your lungs and chest are moving, then you are not breathing properly.

Breathing must include moving the muscles of your abdomen. By raising your abdomen as you breathe, it forces the toxins and stale air in the bottom of your lungs to be expelled. If you take nothing else from this book, learning to breathe properly is the one thing you must learn if being healthy is a priority.

Breathing completely is not just to be done while you do these exercises. It must be done all the time, every breath you take.

Visualizing

Definitions

Before we begin to work with visualizations, I am going to clear up some misconceptions. There is two things of concern at the moment.

First of all: Meditation, Contemplation and Visualization

They are not all the same. These are my definitions.

Meditation is a relatively passive process whereby the "meditator" quiets themselves down and brings themselves into a quiet, meditative state by continually repeating a chosen chant or mantra for a period of time. This person may stop chanting and just remain quiet after the chanting and enjoy being connected to the universe until they choose to return to the mundane world.

Contemplation is a similar process as meditation, except it is slightly more active. In contemplation, the "contemplator" chooses a particular subject they want to connect with and focus on during this process. They could contemplate any subject they choose from "love" to "solving a mystery" in the process of contemplating. The purpose of contemplating is to discover some new knowledge related to the chosen subject.

Visualizations are the most active process of the three. They are often called "Guided Meditations, however; they are not true meditations, as there is an active component to them. There are many, many types of visualizations, such as the ones you are about to learn below.

Visualizations are often tools used for performing esoteric projects. This could include healing facilitation, psychometry, projecting energy, astral projection, and many others.

Guided Meditations are often used as relaxation techniques, or training techniques to help people learn to visualize.

Now, the second definition I am sharing with you is "visualization". This word is an absolute misnomer. According to the word, it means that you need to be able to visualize or "see" what you are working on.

What if you are not a visual person? Does this mean you cannot do visualizations?

The term "visualization" actually refers to "sensing" your way through the process, sensing by whichever tool(s) you choose to use.

You could use any of your senses singly or combined in the process of visualizing. These would include seeing, hearing, feeling non-physically, feeling physically, tasting and smelling. As you become more comfortable working with various visualization processes, you will learn which senses you are most attuned to. None is any better than the other. It is just about getting the job done!

Rules for using Visualizations

One other really important aspect about visualizing. You must let go!

Visualizing is much like mailing a letter. First you recognize the thought that is to become the letter, you write the letter and put it into an envelope, then you put it in the mail box and.... You let it go!

If you miss any one of these steps, you did not complete the task. The universe cannot help you if you are attached to your message.

Next, and just as important... the message must be in present tense. If you send a message to the universe written in future tense, the reply will be... (big universal yawn) "Okay, whenever you are ready, let me know".

When you are doing visualizations, intention is always essential. Visualizations require a clear mind and an open heart. Visualizations only work if the intention is for the absolute good of whom it is intended for, and why it is being projected.

If you just robbed a bank, doing a visualization will not clear your energy field. This process is not a way of escaping self-responsibility.

However, if you or a friend is not feeling well, sending them some energy to help them move their energy to a higher level will work.

It is always best to send energy to others with no expectations. Just like mailing the letter, if you expect something back, you did not let go. Also, if your intention is not honorable, it will not work and may even backfire, causing you repercussions.

Be clear. Be honorable. Let go.

Now, here are some visualizations for your use. Learn the process so you do not have to read it.

Visualizations, even if you do not see them, they are hosted on what is called the "Screen of the mind".

When you are doing the process, pretend there is a movie screen inside the front of your forehead. This is the place where all the activity starts and flows from. Remember to keep yourself separate from the visualization. It is an action. It is not you.

Practical Visualizations

Safety Visualizations

Believing that you are safe on any level is essential to living life fully, and especially when you are working on the esoteric planes.

This visualization is an example of how you can raise your energy to help you feel safe. Please note that it is always up to you to believe that you are safe and to do something about it if you do not feel safe.

Pay attention to your feelings. There may be a learning sitting there for you!

While you are learning how to do this visualization, please sit down somewhere quiet, where you feel safe and comfortable. Once you are more comfortable with the process, you can do it anywhere and anytime you choose. You won't even need to close your eyes. You just do it.

This process can take as long as you choose, and can be repeated as often as you feel necessary.

Here goes!

Safety Cloud

Sit quietly somewhere comfortable. Take a few moments to relax by focusing on your breath. As you relax, visualize yourself immersed in a golden cloud that completely envelopes you. As you breathe, continue to feed more golden light into the cloud, knowing that you are accessing this energy from the Universal Source.

When you feel that your energy has been brought up to an acceptable level, take a deep breath, exhale, and open your eyes.

You can repeat this mantra if you choose: "I know that I am safe and protected". Repeat it at least three times, but you may repeat it as many times as you wish, and as often as you feel you need.

Safety Ring

Same procedure as the Safety Cloud, only visualize a physical ring about 4 feet from your body.

The difference in use between the two visualizations is that the Golden Cloud (preferred) provides the energy for general, non-specific safety as its purpose is to raise your energy. The Golden Ring is used in specific cases when you are putting yourself into a situation of potential danger.

The Golden Ring should only be used in specific situations (of your choice) because it actually limits the flow of Universal Energy in both directions. This limits your ability to send and receive information. It is managed by your ego, as it is a physical protection device.

This process should only be used short term while you physically remove yourself from the situation. It should be used in conjunction with other safety techniques such as feet moving away from the situation.

Once an acceptable distance has been completed, and you feel you can return to safety, do the Safety Cloud in order to raise your energy and get out of fear mode.

Mind and Energy Management Visualizations

If you Google my name on Youtube.com (Monty Ritchings) or on my website: https://powerfulyoupowerfulme.com, you will find at least three videos focused on tools for working with Chakras. Please enjoy them and use them as often as you can.

Opening Your Crown Chakra

The first tool is reconnecting with the Universe when you feel you have become a "head case". To relieve this situation, it is necessary to re-open the Crown Chakra. I will describe it here, however, I truly recommend you view the video.

Touch the pads of your right thumb and right first finger together. Pretend you have a piece of yarn in between your fingers. Raise your right hand about 6"over your head.

Form a circle repeatedly in this position about 4" in diameter in a clockwise direction. Moving slowly wins the race. Repeat this as long as you wish, then lift the end of the yarn up to connect with the Star Chakra, which is about 18" above your head.

Once you have done this, take a deep breath and let go. You just became a "trolley bus", running on Universal Energy.

Remain sitting quietly for a minute and allow yourself to feel the introduction of the energy into your body. Try to feel your mind quieting and your body relaxing.

Once you have completed the visualization, think about something else. Let go!

Managing Your other Chakras.

It is essential for your best health and connection with the Universe that all of your Chakras be open properly and functioning fully. As you learn to experience your own body energy, you will soon be able to feel if a Chakra is open or not.

To open any of the Chakras, just position your hand in the same manner as mentioned above in front of the chosen Chakra. Rotate your hand clockwise slowly for a few seconds. See if you can feel a difference.

For the rear of the Chakra, you will have to do the same exercise except visualize it.

For the Root Chakra, remember to point downward.

Opening the Earth Chakra

Much as opening the Crown Chakra by "reattaching" to the Star Chakra allows you to access sky energy, you can do the same process with the Earth Chakra.

By intentionally connecting with and opening the Earth Chakra, you can help yourself to be more grounded to the earth.

Place your right hand in front of you with your fingers pointing down. Position the pads of your right thumb and first finger together. Move your hand in slow clockwise circles for as long as you choose while mentally connecting with the Earth Chakra.

When you are ready, raise your hand as if you are pulling up the earth energy into your body. Feel it rise into you your feet, legs, body, neck, head and beyond to the Star Chakra.

Release and enjoy the moment of quiet.

73

Chapter 8

Chakras and The Endocrine System

One of the most important concepts that we need to focus on in this discussion is the relationship of the Chakras to the Endocrine System.

What is the Endocrine System?

It is likely the most important system in your body. It is the system that contains any organ or gland that produces chemicals for maintaining Homeostasis. Homeostasis is the process of maintaining metabolic balance in your body, keeping things smooth!

The Endocrine System is your primary protection system. Its purpose is to keep the chemical systems that run in your body regulated so things do not go awry.

However, when the Endocrine system is aroused by an external situation such as stress, anxiety, fear, extreme joy or laughter, it kicks in and releases chemicals that are designed to maintain optimal health.

Another however, if a situation occurs that causes the stimulation to continue for an extended period, problems can arise. If not handled properly, the Endocrine System will continue to attempt to achieve balance.

If the situation continues constantly for months or even years, this can be the beginning of a metabolic imbalance, a disease.

Does all the parts of the Endocrine System kick in when stimulated?

No, the internal memory contained in the egoic mind manages the Endocrine system. The ego is attached to the Endocrine via the emotions.

Ego--------Emotions--------- Endocrine

How does this work?

When we are born, we have pretty much a blank slate in our minds. We have few rules that support us in operating our lives. We need to learn those rules.

How do we learn the rules?

From the time the egg and the sperm meet each other and bond, we begin to learn our own rules of life. During the fetal period, we learn chemically from mom and her environment.

Does dad play a part in this process?

Absolutely! How dad treats mom and interacts with her affects mom, and thus, baby, because mom is emotionally connected to dad. If dad is kind and thoughtful, if he loves rubbing mommy's tummy while she is pregnant, baby thrives. If dad is not so much that way, mom is not happy and baby learns.

When baby is born, the soul enters its body via the opening at the top of the head we call the Crown Chakra, or physically, the pituitary gland. Included with the soul, the baby's mind downloads what information is carried with it from past lives and recent experiences.

The baby now begins learning at a new, independent level. It is separate from mom physically. It is now connected to everyone and everything in its environment, but primarily its family.

Life has begun!

Baby observes, interacts and registers activities that take place around it. It builds its own relationships and belief systems according to its interpretation of the events. These are stored in the egoic mind, now and forever... unless there is intervention.

How does this affect this person in later years?

The developed belief systems do not die away. They can only be replaced by a more dynamic memory. By the time this person is about seven years old, they have created and empowered about ninety percent of their personal belief systems.

Now, as they go about their days, their ego is observing the events as they roll out. When the ego observes a situation that reminds them of a past emotional event, it reacts through the emotions according to the dictates of the related memory. This action causes the Endocrine System to kick in according to its predetermined needs for creating safety in that particular event.

This is often referred to as "Fight or Flight" Syndrome if it is a case that is felt to be negative in nature.

In a positive sense, it could be extreme exultation. Yippee!

Have you ever walked into a room filled with unfamiliar people and found you have an unusual energy exchange with one particular person? The interaction could be one of definite fear and a desire to run away, or a feeling that you want to grab them and run off to the moon.

Both sets of feelings are onset by the memories carried in the ego.

Since you don't have an established relationship with this person, how does this action establish itself?

The Chakras are integrally a part of preset organs in the Endocrine System. Every person has Chakras. They all are actively sending and receiving messages from the world around them all the time.

When a situation such as the above is stimulated, there is an interaction between both persons' energy fields. The information is filtered into the appropriate Chakra, and Voila! A reaction occurs!

The information collected, the Endocrine System, is kicked in by the egoic mind and an appropriate result occurs. Welcome to life!

The relationship between and mastery of the Chakras and the Endocrine system is essential to understand and manage if one wants to live well.

How can one manage the relationship between these two partners?

The first aspect to understand and accept is that even though we have learned some dysfunctional beliefs during our childhood, we are not obligated to believe and accept them over our entire lifetime. We can choose to change and replace them with healthier beliefs.

The most important aspect of this situation is to learn to recognize beliefs that do not help you realize your visualization of your happiest, healthy life.

Working with a good counselor will help you sort out many of these, but being a witness to your own life is the best starting point.

When you realize you are caught up in a situation that goes out of your control; stop, close your eyes (if safe to do so) and do focused tummy based breathing until you return to a quieter level of life.

Just as an add on. Maintaining a healthy flow of chemistry in your body requires developing and maintaining a healthy, positive outlook on life. Breathing correctly, drinking plenty of fresh water, good food and rest are basic requirements.

To stimulate the Endocrine System while exercising, make sure your arms are moving up and down. This is the engine for this system.

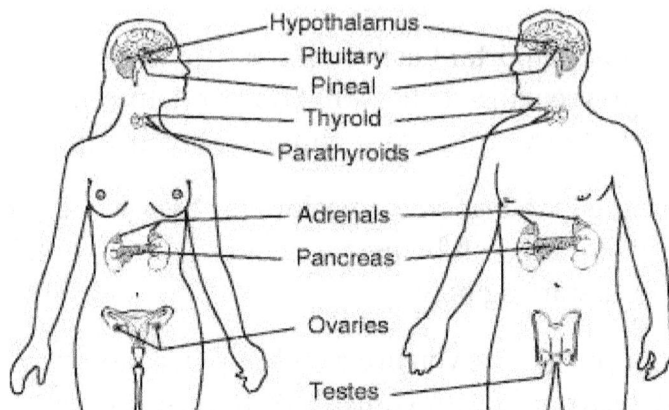

The Endocrine System

Hypothalamus
Pituitary
Pineal
Thyroid
Parathyroids

Adrenals
Pancreas

Ovaries

Testes

The Endocrine System with the Chakras overlayed on the female

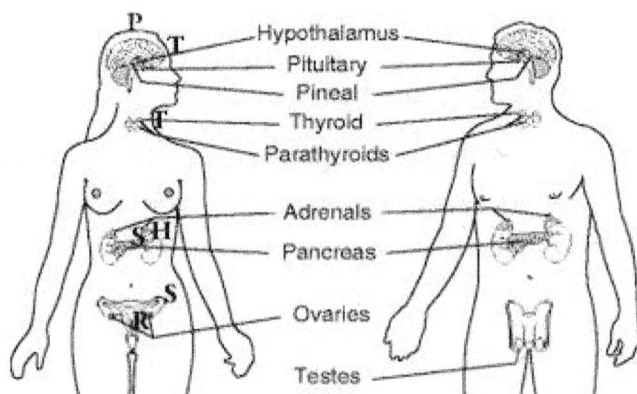

Hypothalamus
Pituitary
Pineal
Thyroid
Parathyroids

Adrenals
Pancreas

Ovaries

Testes

Chapter 9

Summing it up

Free choice is ours at any time about how we live our lives and how we perceive our relationship with everything that exists.

It is possible for us to live our lives completely based in the egoic mind and the physical realm and live a "full" life.

However, we can also choose to see and embrace our life in the greater picture by acknowledging and accepting that the world we live in is much larger than we can perceive through our physical senses.

My hope for you is that by providing the information in this book for your learning pleasure that you will broaden your relationships with all that exist so that you can come to enjoy the real world of Universal Energy.

My intention in providing this information is to help you accept, understand and employ what you have learned in this book into your daily life in the very best, practical way for you to express the amazing person you are.

After all, isn't life about becoming bigger and more real than we have ever been before?

To You

Namaste

Monty

About The Author

Understanding the world we cannot see has been a lifelong passion for me. It just did not make sense that our whole life is based on the physical senses.

The need to understand began as early as I spread my wings as an adult and continues even today, so many, many years later.

From my first experience with the non-physical world through a program called "Mind Dynamics" way back in the 1970s set the course for my life.

My course for making sense of this beautiful world had begun.

Now, with over 30 years as a member of the Rosicrucian Order AMORC as well as innumerable sessions of training in Reiki, Core Belief Engineering, Jin Shin Jyutsu and many others, I offer you this book in hopes that my personal investment in learning the ropes of life will help you to move forward in the Mastery of your Destiny.

Monty lives near Vancouver Canada.

Books by Monty C. Ritchings

Available in all online book stores

Embracing The Blend
What Mom and Dad Didn't Know They Were Teaching You
Description: Understanding how your beliefs develop and run your life, and how to change them. Published 2007 Revised 2009   Revised paperback and Electronic version 2019

Stamp Out Stress
Living With Stress is a Choice, Not a Fact of Life
Description: By ending the war in your mind, you can manage the affairs of your life better by knowing how to manage your stress. Practical tools for mind management.

Paperback Published 2010   Revised Paperback and E-book 2019

Chakras Demystified
Our True Communication System Revealed!

Description: Practical information and tools to help one understand how we communicate on each level of our being and how we can work with them.

Published paperback and Electronically 2019 Revised 2025

Healthy Children Only Need Three Things

Description: Practical insights and tools to enhance our skills in parenting to assist in creating amazing children.

Paperback and Electronically Published 2019

Let's Get Hiking
A Guide For Serious Walkers and Hikers

Helpful tools for successful long distance walking and hiking as well as for international travel

Originally Published Electronically 2015 Revised 2019 Paperback and Electronically published 2023

The Ascenders Return To Grace Book 1

A fun story that provides concepts and tools for attaining higher consciousness
Published in e-book and paperback 2021

The Ascenders Return To Grace Book 2

Continuing story from Book 1 including insights into assisting Mother Nature
Published paperback and e-book 2022

The Ascenders Return To Grace Book 3

Continuing story from Book 2 focused on rewriting DNA as part of raising consciousness
  Published E-book and paperback 2024

The Ascenders Return To Grace
Guide for Thriving in The Age of Aquarius

A guidebook to assist a reader in understanding and implementing the changes available as we move from Pisces to Aquarius

Published E-book and paperback 2024

Mind Management Videos available on YouTube and www.powerfulyoupowerfulme.com/videos

Conscious Mind Management

Living in Present Time

Quieting The Mind